SNAKES!

STRANGE AND WONDERFUL

Laurence Pringle

Illustrated by **Meryl Henderson**

for ———
Laurence Pringle
2015

BOYDS MILLS PRESS
HONESDALE, PENNSYLVANIA

Dedicated to Jeffrey Pringle and Jason Keyes, who apppreciate the beauty and mystery of snakes
                                        —LP

For Ralph, Kim, and Brianna Henderson, who I am proud to call family. Here is another one for your collection.
                                        —MH

The author wishes to thank Kurt Schwenk, PhD, and Charles F. Smith, Department of Ecology and Evolutionary Biology at the University of Connecticut, for reviewing the manuscript and illustrations for accuracy.

Boyds Mills Press, Inc.
815 Church Street
Honesdale, Pennsylvania 18431
Printed in China

Publisher Cataloging-in-Publication Data

Pringle, Laurence P.
    Snakes! : strange and wonderful / by Laurence Pringle :
illustrated by Meryl Henderson. —1st ed.
p. cm.
ISBN: 978-1-59078-003-9 (hc)• ISBN: 978-1-59078-744-1 (pb)
1. Snakes—Juvenile literature. [1. Snakes.]
I. Henderson, Meryl. II. Title.
QL666.O6P75 2004
597.96—dc22
2003026418

First paperback edition, 2009
The text of this book is set in Clearface Regular.
The illustrations are done in watercolor.

10 9 8 7 6 5 4 3 2

Can you eat without using hands?
Snakes can.
Can you climb a tree without using arms or legs?
Snakes can.
Can you smell odors by wiggling your tongue in the air?
Snakes can.

Brazilian rainbow boa—
up to 6 1/2 feet long

3

Snakes can do all these remarkable things, and more. These amazing animals are legless reptiles. Snakes are related to another kind of reptile that *does* have legs—lizards. (In fact, there are legless lizards that look very much like snakes.)

Central bearded dragon— up to 20 inches long

Fraser's scaly-foot (legless lizard)— up to 17¹/2 inches long

Cat-eyed snake—up to 38 inches long

Green anaconda— up to 33 feet long

4

You can find snakes just about everywhere, except in Ireland, Iceland, New Zealand, the Arctic, and on Antarctica. Some are small enough to wrap themselves around your finger. Others are big enough to wrap themselves several times around your whole body.

There are more than two thousand species, or kinds, of snakes. To name a few, there are anacondas, boomslangs, and rosy boas; long-nosed, leaf-nosed, and cat-eyed snakes; parrot, ribbon, and wolf snakes.

Long-nosed tree snake—up to 3 feet long

Madagascan leaf-nose vine snake—up to 35 inches long

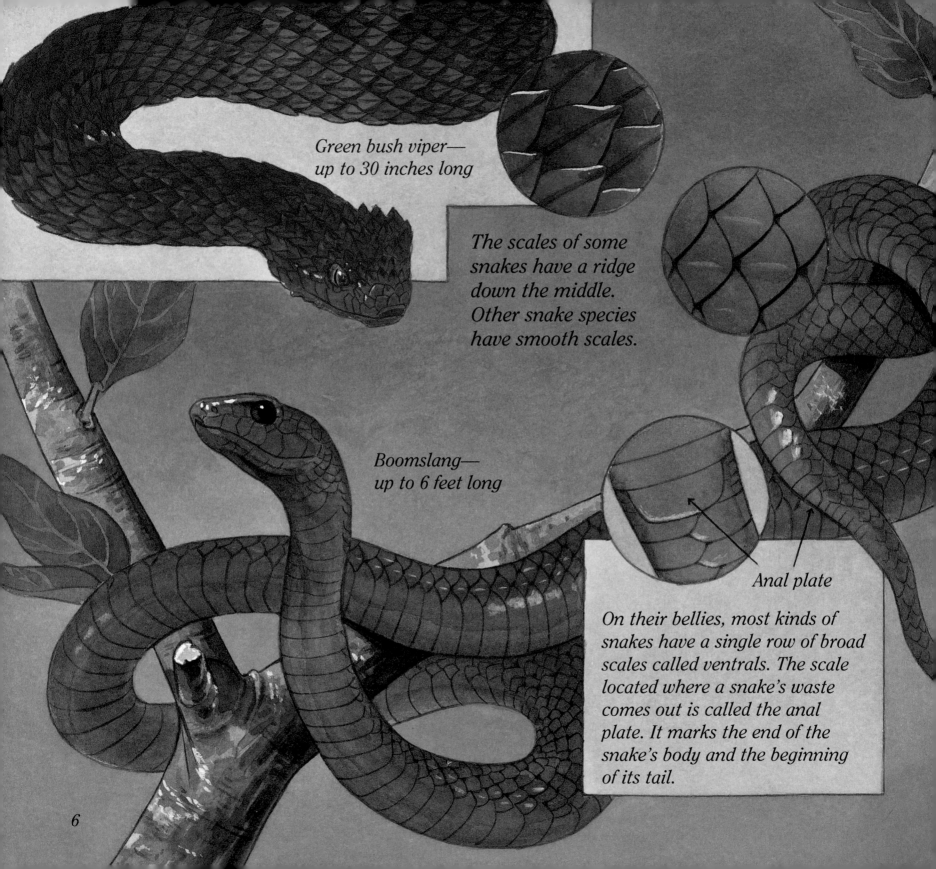

Green bush viper—
up to 30 inches long

The scales of some
snakes have a ridge
down the middle.
Other snake species
have smooth scales.

Boomslang—
up to 6 feet long

Anal plate

On their bellies, most kinds of
snakes have a single row of broad
scales called ventrals. The scale
located where a snake's waste
comes out is called the anal
plate. It marks the end of the
snake's body and the beginning
of its tail.

A few snake species have thick bodies, but most are long and slim. Every snake's body is covered with an outer layer of dry, scaly skin that helps protect it from injury. As a snake grows, it needs a new, roomier skin, so its old skin must be shed. A fast-growing young snake may shed its skin several times in one year.

When a snake is about to shed its skin, it usually stops eating and hides. The clear scales that cover its eyes become cloudy—a sign that the old scaly skin is separating from a fresh new coat of scales underneath.

The snake rubs the sides of its mouth against a rock or other rough surface. The old skin breaks and begins to come loose. Often the snake snags a part of its old skin on a twig or rock, then wriggles away, leaving its old skin in one long piece.

Eastern hognose snake—up to 45 inches long, shedding its skin

Beneath its skin, a snake has strong muscles and many, many bones. Its spine is made up of more than a hundred bones called vertebrae. Some snakes have more than four hundred vertebrae in their bodies and tails. Humans have just thirty-three vertebrae. Humans also have just twenty-four rib bones. A snake has hundreds of rib bones, with a pair attached to each vertebra.

Because it has many vertebrae, a snake can bend in several directions at once, or coil its long body into several tight circles. A snake's twisty body and strong muscles also help it move. This is especially true of sidewinders and other snakes that need to travel on loose or hot surfaces.

A sidewinder hurls its raised head and a loop of its body through the air, landing several inches ahead. Then the front part of the sidewinder serves as an anchor while the snake lifts the rest of its body off the sand to follow the same pathway. Again and again, the snake quickly throws the front part of its body. It skims over the surface, leaving a peculiar trail in the sand.

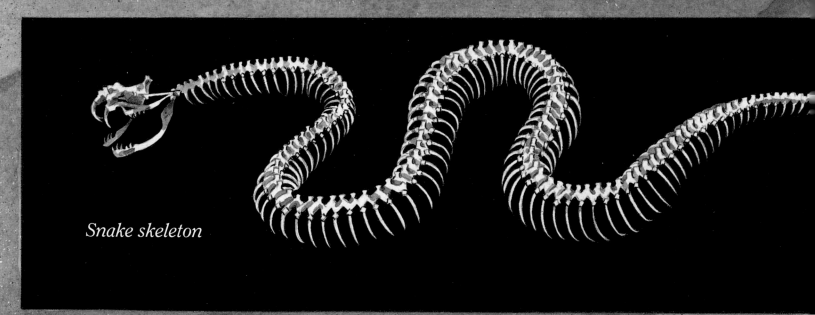

Snake skeleton

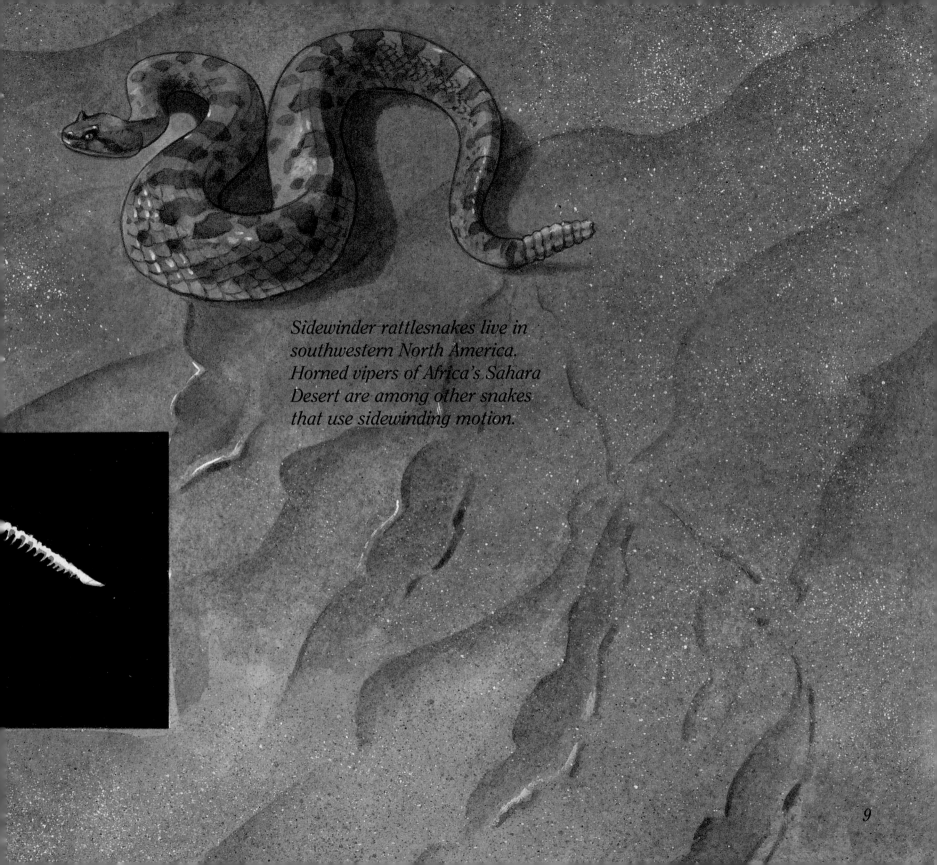

Sidewinder rattlesnakes live in southwestern North America. Horned vipers of Africa's Sahara Desert are among other snakes that use sidewinding motion.

Sometimes a snake creeps along slowly in a straight line. It moves by using the edges of its wide belly scales and strong muscles. Different sections of scales grip the ground while muscles pull those parts of the snake's body forward. Then those scales let go while others hold the ground and muscles pull other body sections forward.

Snakes often travel by making graceful wavelike motions called undulations, using their muscles to push off from the plants, rocks, or bumps on the ground.

A snake can also move by gripping the ground with some curves of its body, then stretching out other parts. This is called concertina movement because the curves of the body are squeezed together, then straightened, like the bellows of a musical instrument called a concertina.

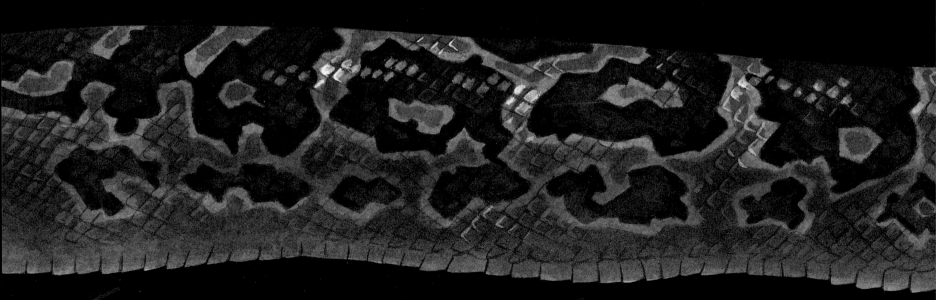

Creeping movement

*African rock python—
up to 23 feet long*

Undulating movement

Concertina movement

11

Paradise flying snake—
up to 4 feet long

Carpet python—
up to 13 feet long

Without legs, snakes can creep, slither, and even race over the ground. Snakes called racers can travel at almost four miles an hour, while black mambas move at seven miles an hour. Snakes can also climb and swim, and a few species can glide through the air.

A snake climbs by gripping part of a tree trunk with some of its muscles and scales while the rest of its body stretches upward. Then its front section holds on while the rear part is pulled up.

All snakes can swim, but the best swimmers are sea snakes, which live in the South Pacific and Indian oceans. They swim well because their tails are flattened, like canoe paddles. They can dive deeply and stay underwater for more than an hour. More than fifty kinds of sea snakes live on Earth. They live in the warm water of salt marshes, in mangrove swamps, and in coral reefs. Some sea snakes swim in the open ocean and never come near land.

On the island of Borneo and other places in Southeast Asia, you may see snakes in the air. Flying snakes hunt for lizards high in trees. As a snake launches itself into the air, it flattens its body so it is shaped like a long ribbon. It steers by moving its tail and by making undulation movements as it glides to another tree or to the ground.

Pelagic sea snake—
up to 5 feet long

As snakes move or lie in wait to catch some food, their senses stay alert. However, their eyesight is usually not strong. It is best at spotting an animal moving nearby.

Snakes also hear very poorly. They have no ear openings or eardrums but do have inner ears. Snakes can detect low-frequency sounds in the air. They can also feel vibrations from the ground caused by the footsteps of a moving animal.

When a snake sticks out its tongue at you, it is not being mean. It is trying to learn about you with its sense of smell. It also takes in odors through its nostrils, as you do, but its tongue gives the snake more information about scents. Both tips of the forked tongue collect odor particles from the air. When the snake's tongue is pulled back into its mouth, bits of odor are passed along to special scent-detecting organs. One of the two tips may collect more odor particles than the other. This tells the snake whether the scent is coming from its left or right.

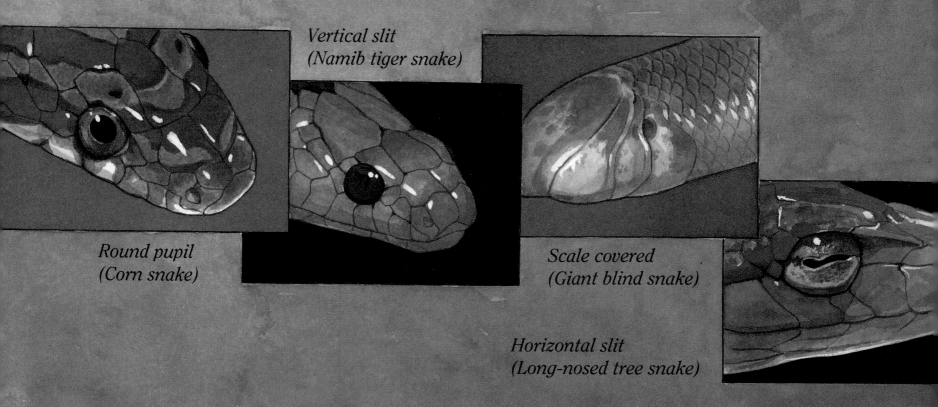

Round pupil
(Corn snake)

Vertical slit
(Namib tiger snake)

Scale covered
(Giant blind snake)

Horizontal slit
(Long-nosed tree snake)

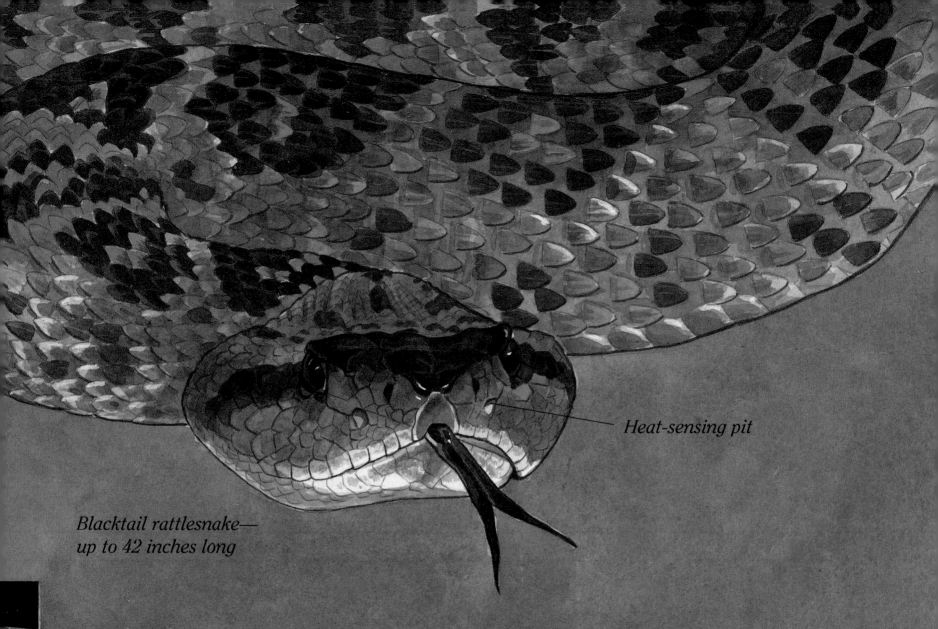

Heat-sensing pit

*Blacktail rattlesnake—
up to 42 inches long*

Some kinds of snakes can detect the heat given off by the body of a live animal. Rattlesnakes have heat-sensing cells in two small pits located between their eyes and their nostrils. They belong to a group of snakes called pit vipers. After a rattlesnake gives a poisonous bite to a small mammal, its prey may run on for a while before dying. Flicking its tongue in the air, the snake follows the animal's scent trail and finds its dead prey.

All snakes swallow their food whole, without chewing. Small snakes catch little animals, such as earthworms, insects, and mice. The smallest snakes known, called thread snakes, are only a few inches long and eat the eggs and pupae of ants and termites. The biggest snakes, including pythons and anacondas, have been known to eat deer and pigs.

Some snakes have special diets, and special ways of getting the foods they like. Snail-eating snakes are able to pull snails from their shells. Other kinds of snakes eat only centipedes or eels or toads. The king cobra eats other snakes! And in Africa and India there are snakes that eat only bird eggs.

Large or small, a snake sometimes catches an animal that may seem too big to be swallowed. But most kinds of snakes have upper and lower jaws that are loosely joined, and the two halves of their lower jaws can also stretch apart. So snakes can open their mouths wide . . . Wider . . . WIDER—and swallow animals that are two or three times wider than their heads.

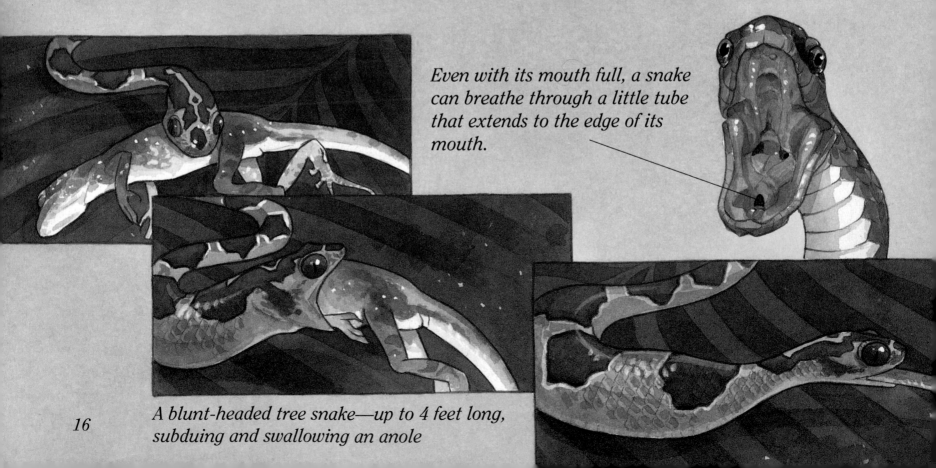

Even with its mouth full, a snake can breathe through a little tube that extends to the edge of its mouth.

A blunt-headed tree snake—up to 4 feet long, subduing and swallowing an anole

Indian rock python— up to 23 feet long, swallowing a pig

The king cobra, up to 17 feet long, is Earth's biggest venomous snake.

Many kinds of snakes first grab their prey with their teeth, then quickly wrap coils of their bodies around the animal. This protects the snake from the struggling animal's teeth and claws. The snake then tightens its coils, minute after minute, until the pressure on the prey's chest causes its heart to stop working. After the animal dies, the snake loosens its grip and eats its meal.

A snake that squeezes its prey to death is called a constrictor. All of Earth's biggest snakes—boas, pythons, and anacondas—are constrictors.

Yellow anaconda—
up to 10 feet long,
constricting a caiman

*McGregor's pit viper—
up to 3 feet long,
about to strike a
common flying dragon*

Venom gland

*Hollow
fang*

Pit viper's venom system

20

About 450 of the 2,700 species of snakes on Earth kill their prey by injecting a venom with their teeth. Some venoms harm an animal's nervous system and cause its heart and lungs to stop working. Others damage an animal's muscles or its blood and blood-circulating system.

Venomous snakes have fangs on their upper jaws that are connected to glands that produce venom. Cobras, coral snakes, and sea snakes hold their prey with their teeth while they inject venom. When a rattlesnake or other pit viper stabs its fangs into the body of an animal, muscles around the glands squeeze venom through the hollow fangs. Then the snake lets go, and its fangs fold back against the roof of its mouth.

Humans are not the usual prey of any snake, but snakes may bite people in self-defense. About three hundred snake species have venom that can kill a person. Sea snake venom is especially strong, but these snakes rarely bite people. Even when they bite in self-defense, they may not release their venom. Some other venomous snakes are more aggressive—and deadly. People can be saved from a venomous bite if medicines called antivenoms are available and given in time. Still, snakebites kill several thousand people each year, especially in India, Africa, and South America.

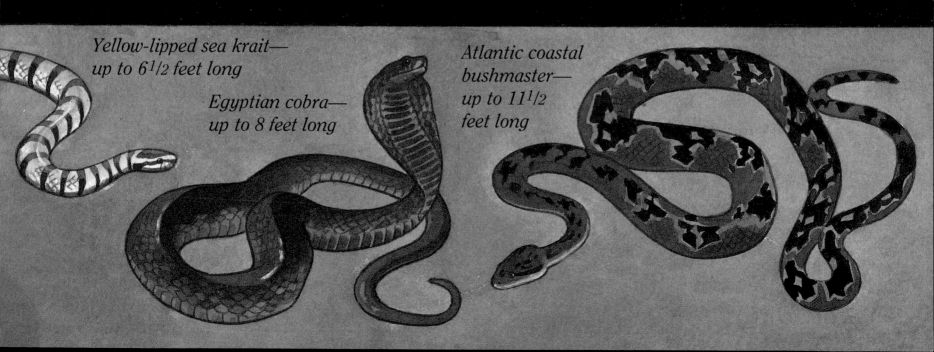

Yellow-lipped sea krait— up to 6¹/₂ feet long

Egyptian cobra— up to 8 feet long

Atlantic coastal bushmaster— up to 11¹/₂ feet long

BBBBBBBZZZZZZ! The whirring buzz of a rattlesnake's rattle is a warning to stay away. The noise helps protect the snake from large animals that might step on it by accident.

Each time a rattlesnake sheds its skin, a hollow hard piece remains at the tip of its tail. Some of these pieces break off, but a rattlesnake usually has enough to make its warning sound by shaking its tail.

About thirty different kinds of rattlesnakes live in North America. They are related to other kinds of pit vipers that live in North America—copperheads and moccasins—that do not have rattles. Coral snakes also have venomous bites and live in North America. They are related to cobras and sea snakes. The bright colors of a coral snake are a sign: Danger! Keep Away!

Cross-section view of rattle

Western diamondback rattlesnake—up to 6 feet long

Copperhead—up to 4 feet long

Water moccasin (cottonmouth)—
up to 6 feet long

Eastern coral Snake—
up to 3 feet long

23

The scales of most snakes have colors and patterns that help them hide in their usual habitats. Tree and vine snakes are often colored green. Snakes that wait to catch animals on the forest floor can blend in among fallen leaves.

Five snakes are shown on these pages. They are the copperhead and the rough green snake of North America, the Gaboon viper of Africa, the white-lipped pit viper of Asia, and the leaf-nose snake of Madagascar. Can you find them?

Rosy boa—up to 3¹/₂ feet long

On a summer day, you may see a snake warming itself in the sun. If its body temperature rises too high, the snake retreats to the shade. It must get out of the sun in order to keep a steady body temperature. Snakes get most of their body warmth from their surroundings. They are ectothermic, which means "outside heat." (Humans, other mammals, and birds are endothermic, which means "inside heat.")

As autumn days grow shorter and cooler in the north, snakes become less active. They seek a safe place to survive the cold of winter, an underground den where they stay until spring. In some areas, hundreds of snakes of different kinds gather together deep in rocky caves.

Thousands of red-sided garter snakes travel as far as twenty miles to reach their winter den in Manitoba, Canada. It is the world's largest gathering of snakes. They emerge in the spring, mate, and spread out into the countryside.

Red-sided garter snakes in winter den—up to 4 feet long

After a male and female snake mate, baby snakes begin to develop inside the female's body. Boas, rattlesnakes, and garter snakes give birth to live young. The babies develop completely inside their mother and are born surrounded with a thin membrane. With a small, temporary tooth on their snouts—called an egg tooth—they cut through the membrane and wriggle free.

Many other kinds of snakes lay eggs. Female coral snakes and racers search for a safe, warm hiding place for their eggs. The mother leaves, never to return, after laying her eggs. Weeks later, the young snakes slit their shells open with an egg tooth, then begin to hunt for their first meal.

Some mother snakes stay with their eggs. Female king cobras build nests of dead leaves for their eggs, and guard them. Some female pythons also stay with their eggs. A mother python coils her body around her eggs and shivers. This warms her body, which then helps keep the eggs warm. For many weeks she cares for her eggs in this way. Once her young hatch, they are on their own.

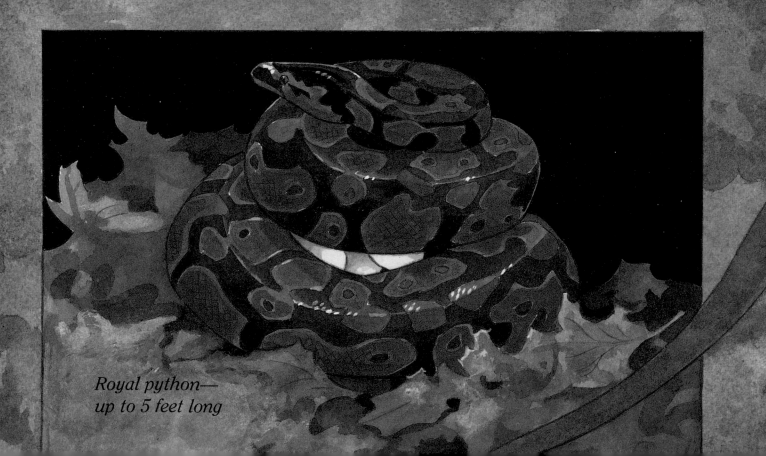

*Royal python—
up to 5 feet long*

Hognose viper—up to 32 inches long, giving birth

Young in membrane

*Red-sided garter snake—
up to 4 feet long*

30

Leaving its mother or egg, a young snake crawls into a new and dangerous world. Some people try to kill any snake they see. Many animals hunt and eat both young and adult snakes. A hawk may swoop down, clutch a snake in its talons, and carry it back to its nest. Crows, foxes, raccoons, and coyotes also eat snakes.

Snakes themselves eat all sorts of smaller animals, including mice, rats, and other rodents that are sometimes pests of humans. Snakes are an important part of many food webs in nature.

Even though most snakes are harmless to humans, some people feel uncomfortable with their slithering way of moving, their unblinking eyes, and their flicking forked tongues. Other people look at them and see graceful beauty and feel curiosity about lives so different from their own.

Snakes are truly strange and wonderful!

*Scarlet kingsnake—
up to 27 inches long,
killing and eating a mouse*

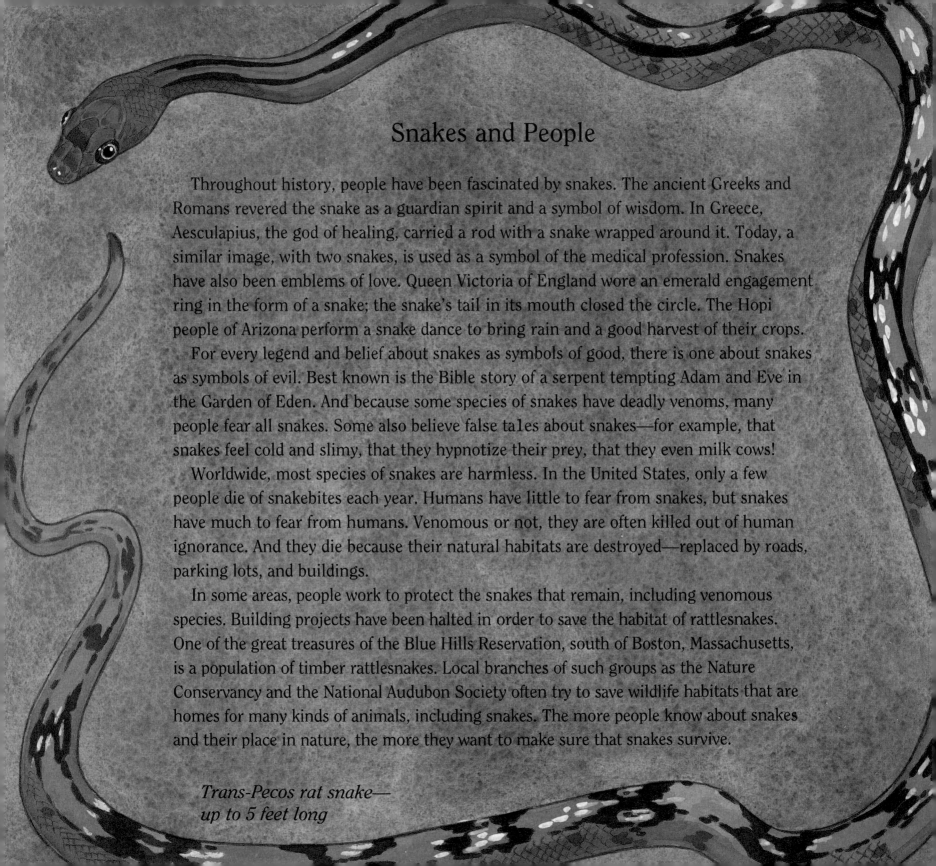

Snakes and People

Throughout history, people have been fascinated by snakes. The ancient Greeks and Romans revered the snake as a guardian spirit and a symbol of wisdom. In Greece, Aesculapius, the god of healing, carried a rod with a snake wrapped around it. Today, a similar image, with two snakes, is used as a symbol of the medical profession. Snakes have also been emblems of love. Queen Victoria of England wore an emerald engagement ring in the form of a snake; the snake's tail in its mouth closed the circle. The Hopi people of Arizona perform a snake dance to bring rain and a good harvest of their crops.

For every legend and belief about snakes as symbols of good, there is one about snakes as symbols of evil. Best known is the Bible story of a serpent tempting Adam and Eve in the Garden of Eden. And because some species of snakes have deadly venoms, many people fear all snakes. Some also believe false tales about snakes—for example, that snakes feel cold and slimy, that they hypnotize their prey, that they even milk cows!

Worldwide, most species of snakes are harmless. In the United States, only a few people die of snakebites each year. Humans have little to fear from snakes, but snakes have much to fear from humans. Venomous or not, they are often killed out of human ignorance. And they die because their natural habitats are destroyed—replaced by roads, parking lots, and buildings.

In some areas, people work to protect the snakes that remain, including venomous species. Building projects have been halted in order to save the habitat of rattlesnakes. One of the great treasures of the Blue Hills Reservation, south of Boston, Massachusetts, is a population of timber rattlesnakes. Local branches of such groups as the Nature Conservancy and the National Audubon Society often try to save wildlife habitats that are homes for many kinds of animals, including snakes. The more people know about snakes and their place in nature, the more they want to make sure that snakes survive.

Trans-Pecos rat snake—
up to 5 feet long